# Cheese Dome Power

**by kac young**
PhD, DCH, ND, RScM

Published  by Marlene Morris Ministries, Inc.
Cover design: Marlene Morris
Illustrations: kac young
Back cover photo: Marlene Morris
ISBN:978-098-1836881
First printing June 2011
Second Printing 2019

**Cheese Dome Testimonials:**

*What a sweet and novel idea - and one that really works! If you're looking for healing in some area of your life - and who isn't? - by all means, read this book. The magic - or whatever it is! - worked for the author of this lovely book - Kac Young - and it will work for you, too. Me? I'm sold! I loved this book and so will you.* **J. Randy Taraborrelli, New York Times' Best-Selling Author**

*The Cheese Dome is a wonderful symbol of the healing power of love. Knowing that a friend has placed you in his or her sphere of concern, loving wishes and prayer gives you hope and confidence all will end well. Then it does!* **Margaret Kent, Author, Best Selling Author New York Times,** *How To Marry The Man of Your Choice,*

*I was so inspired after reading this book I acquired a cheese dome of my own the same day! Dr. young's experiences with the power of the cheese dome remind us that the Universe is an ally and not an enemy.* **Craig Dublin Macmillan, Educator**

*At a time in the world where there is little hope, it is such an inspiration to read something that gives us hope and positive thoughts and a place to go when we need help.* **Carolyn Lombardo, Hollywood Television Caterer**

*In Cheese Dome Power we learn about its mysterious power to facilitate healing. We meet some extraordinary friends and some of their special domes. Finally, we are encouraged to become a power for gouda. Be careful – this little book could change your life.* **Richard Morgan, CFO**

*This fun and intriguing book describes how a simple Cheese Dome can change your life for the better. And it works - I can testify to that!"Cheese Dome Power can change your life! In this delightful book, kac, with her inimitable eloquence, wit and humor, describes how we can all tap into the magical power of the Cheese Dome to heal our lives and realize our dreams. And it works - I can testify to that! A few days after experiencing the benevolence of kac's Cheese Dome I found one of my very own (or should I say it found me?). It's rapidly being filled with requests from friends who are now determined to acquire their own Cheese Domes. Read this book, find a Cheese Dome and have fun manifesting!* **Lisa Tenzin-Dolma, Author, Artist, Singer**

*Cheese Dome Power is the manual of how to harness your fretting and angst into something positive and powerful to make those wanted changes in your life. And it's much safer than lighting candles!!! Cheese Dome Power is a great way to help yourself and those you love.*
**Kool Marder, Film Producer, Hollywood**

*Busy hands doing the work of angels.* **Fred Kepler, Editor**

*There have been many books on spirituality and prayer but few also offer humor. Kac Young's Cheese Dome offers readers a new road to belief while at the same time accessing whimsy. Once the reader has completed the book they will be scouring eBay for their own Cheese Dome. What a joyous thought indeed!* **Tracy Abbott Cook, former writer The Tonight Show with Jay Leno, Late Night With David Letterman**

*This book is a wonderfully fun read. Kac Young's energy, wit and positive spirit shine through every page. I have to admit that I find the whole idea pretty wacky, but I certainly hope my name and my husband's are under that cheese dome!* **Donna Wells, prominent Los Angeles Westside attorney and former General Counsel to the California Film Commission**.

*Prepare to welcome the newest member of your family: the Cheese Dome! This inspirational gem will renew your faith in the power of the universe and have you laughing out loud. Buy this book, head to your local thrift store or a garage sale, and get ready to watch your life improve! It's as easy as 1-2-3!*
**Leola Dublin Macmillan, Critical Essayist and PhD candidate**

Dedicated to: **Peggy Jones**
the founder of the original healing Cheese Dome, my very best friend and an inspiration to everyone she touches.

## Acknowledgements:

My love and gratitude to the amazing Marlene Morris for her incredible support, sense of humor, encouragement and graphic design talents without whom this book would still be sitting on a tea stained yellow pad with upturned corners. (Thank you!)

My endless love and appreciation to Pamela Ventura and her unbelievable support for the Cheese Dome, her contributions to this effort and her total belief in the results of this miracle maker.

My heart and soul appreciation to Lisa Tenzin-Dolma for encouraging me with this book, for her faith in the Cheese Dome and her delightful sense of humor that keeps me energized and focused, always.

Very special gratitude to Shell Kepler for her inspiration, her friendship, her contagious laugh and all the vivid memories I have of her courage, charisma and spirit.

And to all the Cheese Domes in the world, sitting in secondhand shops, waiting patiently for their new owners to come along. Have faith little ones, your day is coming.

## Table of Contents

## Introduction

We're all blessed in so many ways in our lives and challenged in other ways, too. One of my many blessings is my long-time friendship with Peggy Jones. We have laughed together, cried together and probably had as much fun as is legally allowed, which is a good thing since her husband is in law enforcement. Peggy discovered the first healing Cheese Dome. It was her innovation and she passed it on to me. My job is to pass it along to you so that this amazing tool can help you live your life with more love, more joy and more healing than you ever imagined.

I wish you a best friend as wonderful as Peggy, and I enthusiastically pass on to you the information about Cheese Dome Power so that you may discover the awesome power in having a Cheese Dome of your very own.

The stories are all true, I've changed a few names and places to protect privacy, but most came forth in strength and numbers to testify to the veracity of the Cheese Dome.

I hope you'll join us.

## Chapter One: Genesis

*In the Beginning God created the heaven and the earth. And the earth was without form and void and darkness was upon the face of the deep.*[1] In 1991 that pretty much summed up my life: seriously out of form, dark and void. It hadn't always been so. The events leading up to the dark and void were the stuff of which nightmares or horror films are made. A good title might have been: *Backstage at the Ten Most Horrendous Home Owning Experiences.*

It all began innocently, with the idea of adding a second story to my home. On paper this looked like (according to the beautiful sketches), and sounded like (according to the estimate), a really good idea.

It turns out that good ideas and reality are not necessarily soul mates. The builder's budget was a fantasy. The building schedule was like a vaudeville comedy sketch (and the workers probably should have been in rehab). And apparently the workers thought they knew more than the weatherman (who had predicted storm warnings for intense spring showers) when they left any hint of covering off the house after they had removed the entire roof.

---

[1] Holy Bible, King James Version, Genesis 1:1

On the wettest May weekend in the history of Los Angeles, I watched the ceilings of my house cave in one after another as hundreds of gallons of water poured from the sky. It was as if a careless Archangel had mistakenly left a hose running in his celestial backyard pool. As the water flowed from the sky, the ceilings crumbled, and my hardwood floors almost instantly warped into curved planks resembling the sides of Noah's Ark. My furniture was covered in water-sogged, thick, gooey plaster that had once been original 1938 hand-crafted construction, and every carpet, piece of clothing, computer gadget, office supply or kitchen utensil was smothered in overly irrigated, collapsed ceiling residue.

I stood in my formerly beautiful sanctuary dumbstruck. This couldn't be happening.

During the same timeframe, my father had become very ill, the television show I was directing had been cancelled, the man I thought I was going to marry went back to his estranged wife. I was supposed to be escaping the scourges of reality the next day on a European vacation. The plan was that the builder and team would finish the expansion and remodel while I was off creating a new love in my life and healing my wounds.

I watched as my life plans and my house disappeared down a metaphorical drain in under 30 minutes. Looming in my shell-shocked brain was the new question: where was I going to live now that I literally had no roof over my head and the prospects for acquiring one within a reasonable time seemed more remote than Europe and less likely than mending my broken heart abroad.

The torrential rain had shut the power down. There were no lights by which to investigate any more of the damage, so I grabbed my packed-for-Europe bags with me and headed for a hotel. I stopped for some wine on the way. As I removed my drenched clothing and peeled the plaster pieces out of my sorry, sick and sad ceiling-soaked hair, I drank Cabernet from a hotel plastic cup and phoned my best friend Peggy.

Between gulps of wine I sobbed my woes across the long-distance lines. She said, "Oh dear," followed by a comforting "there, there," and, "it will all be alright." "No, it won't," I wailed, "My whole house is gone, what am I going to do?"

In her most soothing and comforting voice she replied, "Wait just a minute, I'm going to put you in the Cheese Dome." "The what?" I asked. "The healing Cheese Dome," she said, as if I was supposed to know what *that* was. But that is exactly what is so endearing about Peggy.

In the midst of a hideous personal crisis, she thinks of cheese. "What kind of cheese is in there?" I asked limply. My traumatized brain wondered if there were cheese domes in Europe. "No cheese in the dome," Peggy replied, "just people." It was the worst day of my life and my best friend in the whole world wanted to put me under glass. What's the world coming to? I sobbed some more.

"*Shhhhh,*" cooed Peggy. So I "shhhhed." As I listened, I learned that my name was going to be written on a slip of paper and placed under the cover of what was once a receptacle for cheese, but which was apparently currently experiencing some kind of second life as a healer. Somehow, when Peggy explained it to me, it made sense. Of course, I *had* been through a horrific day.

Under the Healing Cheese Dome, my peace was slipped with a promise from Peggy that I would have healing powers circulating around me and coursing through my life 24/7. I needn't worry further about a thing because the "*Power of the Cheese Dome will fix everything.*" Those thoughts helped dry my tears, pat my head, and soothe my straggly hair from 1600 miles away. I was a purring kitten by the time I settled into my hotel bed comforted by the calming security of my expectations from the Healing Cheese Dome.

The next morning, I awoke to the hotel phone ringing off the hook at 6 AM. My serenity was jolted sharply by the builder who wanted to know what he should do next. "Should I *really* tell him," I thought to myself as I bit my tongue. It was Sunday of Memorial Day weekend and we had to wait another two days before I could call my insurance company to send an adjuster out to what was left of my house, to assess the damages. My head was swimming with "what if's" but I agreed to meet the builder at the house in two hours. I suggested he call *his* insurance guy, too, as the fault was fairly clearly on the shoulder of his negligent workers.

Thoughts of the Cheese Dome disappeared during the exhausted depths of a good night's sleep. I hustled my bustle up to the house, wearing two layers from my Europe-bound summer wardrobe and surveyed, with overwhelming horror, the rest of the damage that had occurred.

My home looked like a bombed-out village from a WWII movie. Everything was in shambles. I gathered up some clothes, wet and gnarly as they were, grabbed my soggy Day Planner (it was 1991) a stack of yellow pads, and my insurance policy and headed back to the hotel to start making lists while I waited for Tuesday morning and the opening of my insurance agent's office.

By 10 AM Tuesday morning troops were mustered, and events began happening at the speed of exploding Chinese firecrackers. Adjusters were swarming, heads were shaking, pencil leads were breaking and suddenly I was surrounded by a team of "restoration" people who were asking me, in three different languages, what I wanted to do with all my "stuff".

There were three trucks: one was for "storage" (*long term* was becoming apparent), one was for "trash", and the third was for my new apartment. New apartment? Holy Shish kabobs, I hadn't even thought about that! Of course, I needed to rent an apartment...where else was I going to live now that my former home had become a candidate for leading horror story of the year.

The day was long and by the end of it I had no voice. I had decided the fate of everything I owned in less than 8 hours and one truck was waiting for me to tell it where it should deliver my surviving furniture and dripping wet possessions. I hadn't had time to find a dry newspaper let alone search for an apartment to rent, so we agreed that I would "call them" when I knew where I was going to live and then they could deliver my things.

As luck would have it, I drove down the hill and found an "apartment for rent" sign and the manager was in. I spoke of my instantaneous need for an apartment and, after running a quick credit check, and signing my life away for a six-month minimum lease, she handed me the keys to a lovely 3-bedroom apartment.

Wow, I had a home. Back to the hotel I went and after consuming some easily accessed take out, I called Peggy. *"My poor sweet friend,"* she said, and I felt instantaneously better.

Then she said, *"See the Cheese Dome power is kicking in. Look at all you did in 24 hours."* Huh? I hadn't stopped long enough to appreciate all that had been accomplished. Maybe she was right. Maybe it was the Cheese Dome helping me. But that's so silly. I dismissed it immediately and credited my television producing skills and gift of organization for surviving the day with my mind intact and no bodies to bury.

Months passed and I was still in my apartment observing the construction. What had originally been the addition of a top floor, was now the reconstruction of an entire two-story dwelling from the foundation up. The costs skyrocketed and the insurance companies went at each other like two stray cats over a bucket of KFC's finest. I stayed out of the mess referring each one to the other and prayed for a quick settlement.

Construction was constantly being held up because of late insurance payments and I eventually discovered that the "restoration company" was not quite as *on the level* as one would have hoped. Many of my possessions, it seemed, had mysteriously "disappeared" in transit.

The longer the delays, the more the costs soared, the more hair I tore out, the more slips of paper Peggy put under the Cheese Dome. Weeks turned into months and then finally, one year later, I moved back home. The new copper pipes gleamed, the fresh electric wires hummed happily carrying current to the updated light fixtures, the new floors shone like a basketball court and the carpet was spanking new. Euphoria. I called Peggy from the newly reinstated phone line and, two states apart, and we celebrated. Peggy lifted the Cheese Dome in honor of all its accomplishments and we were happy.

We both agreed that so many things could have gone wrong, so much else could have happened, but the healing power of the Cheese Dome somehow settled the disputes and made it all work. I was willing to give it credit.

That Christmas Peggy sent me my very own Cheese Dome. "It is time," she said, "for you to have your own and use it to help other people heal." Wow! My very own healing Cheese Dome.

I stared at it in the box for several days until I got the gumption to open it. "Welcome to your new home in Hollywood," I whispered to the Cheese Dome as I gingerly unwrapped its parts. There it was in all its mysterious glory; a shiny bright glass Cheese Dome sitting in my kitchen just waiting for the first healing need. *"There's some kind of strange power in that Cheese Dome,"* I thought to myself. *"I don't understand it, but there's power in it for sure."*

The phone rang. It was my friend Pamela and she was upset and sounded desperate. "Those bastards," were the first words out of her mouth.

## Chapter Two: Pamela's Truth

Kac came into my life as a bonus when I married my husband. The two of them have been friends for many years and are more like brother and sister than many full-blooded brothers and sisters I know. Our association has been long and happy, and we've been through many ups and downs together, always offering some kind of help – be it physical, psychological, spiritual or philosophical.

A few years ago, my previously happy work world disintegrated into a hideous hellhole of horror. The once delightful Hollywood studio that employed me turned into a salt mine headed by slave drivers whose only concern was for the almighty dollar. Gone was the old familial feeling; replaced by new and bewildering job assignments, long (and unpaid) hours at our desks and at home, and dark stretches of time when husbands, wives and children didn't see our faces.

When we were able to be with our loved ones we were so tired and cranky that they probably preferred the alternative option.

There were many casualties resulting from this shoddy treatment, and I was determined not to be one of them. Raised with a staunch work ethic and the belief that I could do anything I put my mind to, I resolved to triumph over the adversity that was my job.

After a year or so of being unsuccessful at this quest, I became depressed and withdrawn and my darling husband probably thought his wife had been switched in the night with one of the Gorgons from mythology. My health was suffering, my brain was inside out, and life was fetid.

I called my friend, Kac, knowing that she'd have some great words or a witty repartee that would at least make me laugh and at best give me some insight as to how to cope. What I got from her was, "I'll put you in The Cheese Dome."

At first I questioned whether or not she'd had too many glasses of the red wine we often shared and wondered if she was kidding. No, she assured me, the new Cheese Dome was waiting on her kitchen counter and it was just the ticket to relief for me. She would put me inside and the Dome would work its magic and my problems would be resolved.

OK, I thought…'cheese' sounds kind of similar to 'Jesus' and 'dome' is remarkably similar to 'Om," the sacred chant of several Eastern religions. Perhaps it's some symbiotic combination of the two that makes it work. Or maybe it's like Pyramid Power, wherein the peak of the pyramid focuses energy down onto whatever is inside it.

The difference between the peak and the dome would be that the dome's energy would be softer and more rounded…focused like the sunlight through the convex lens of those magnifying glasses we used to use to set leaves on fire when we were kids.[2] That or Kac had misplaced a few important marbles. Either way, it couldn't hurt.

So Kac put me into the Cheese Dome and I waited to see what would happen. The Dome-itude is not something that is instantaneous, mind you. The energy swirls around and gathers more goodness from the cosmos and gives you time to try to work things out yourself, all the while knowing that you're getting help from the Dome. It's like a booster shot of karma or something.

Eventually I found a way to deal with my employment situation that was not only a blessing for me mentally and physically, it was a very satisfying end to the rapaciousness and greed of my former employer's attitude – at least on a departmental level. The Dome gave me the fortitude and determination to fight the good fight and help lots of other people who had been taken advantage of, and some of the Coffers of the Evil Empire were drained and the spoils were spread amongst those deserving of restitution.

---

[2] And that fire at the playground had nothing to do with me!

So, I'm grateful to the Cheese Dome for whatever it is that it does, whether it is swirling cosmic energy or combining the power of Jesus, Om, and I'm sure many other spiritual doctrines, for those of us who just need a little something extra to focus us.

## Chapter Three: Peggy Discovers the Secret Power of the Healing Cheese Dome

Cheese Dome healings all began with Peggy Jones in Vancouver, Washington. In 1990 her children were leaving the nest and beginning lives of their own. She ached with a mother's concern as they moved out and moved on, leaving her watchful guidance and gentle curfews. Would they be alright? Would they get enough rest? Would they know how to care for a cold? Would they eat right? Would someone break their hearts? She wanted to *be* there for them to help them make their way in the world, yet she knew she had to let them go.

At the same time that Peggy was losing sleep over her children, a close friend of hers was taking a class called, *"The Secret Place: Finding Your Inner Sanctuary."* The class coached her in creating a confidential place in consciousness where she would experience herself as loved, safe, protected and divinely guided. She was trained in the spiritual ways of being able to go to this safe place anytime she wanted or needed to. In the safety of this sanctuary, she could meet with anyone she choose to, ask them any questions she had on her mind, and avail herself of their wisdom. If she wanted to speak with Gandhi; she could. If she preferred the Archangel Michael; he was available. Anybody from any time period would show up just for the asking. All of her mysteries would be solved, her anxieties calmed, and her purpose defined.

This sacred space was open to her all of the time. She was encouraged to invite others to join her: providing them the same private sanctuary. Her friend relayed the process to Peggy. In an instant Peggy connected with the information and thought she might be able to protect her children and help them find their way in the world by taking them to *her* secret place, without them even knowing it. The question in her mind was *how* to accomplish that. The answer arose from a very unlikely incident.

One weekend, her neighbor had a garage sale. It had poured earlier that morning and a few items were soaking wet, but the newspaper ads had enticed the locals so much that everyone arrived eager to buy (from under the shelter of their umbrellas.) They came in droves and purchased the treasures, soggy or not. Typical of garage sales, at the end of the day there were still  items which remained unsold. A rain sprinkled Cheese Dome was among them. It was perched on the corner of a display table and looked only slightly worse for the weather and the wear.

The Cheese Dome caught Peggy's eye and she just knew she had to buy it. Confident that she had found the answer to her haunting question, she handed her neighbor four quarters and transported the Cheese Dome under her raincoat across the road to its new home.

Half an hour later, washed, polished and spotless, the Cheese Dome sat on her counter. Peggy stared at it for a long while and wondered to herself why it had spoken so loudly to her. "What did this all mean?" she thought to herself. "It's a safe place," was the answer she got. It made complete sense. The dome that had protected cheese from the perils of the environment (and curious perpetrators) radiated safety and security. From now on it would be her secret place. No longer charged with protecting ordinary cheese against would be marauders, this Cheese Dome with its gleaming glass dome fitting snugly into a carved groove on its wooden support, had a new purpose. It would become a sacred custodian for those who needed comfort and restoration. That night she slept like a baby.

Once anointed, the Cheese Dome quickly became a haven for torn slips of paper, business cards, photographs and special requests which represented the hopes, dreams, perils and challenges of everyone Peggy loved. Peggy put each of her children in the Cheese Dome knowing they were now fully protected.

As Peggy relayed her story to friends and acquaintances, the requests to be placed in the Cheese Dome multiplied like rabbits at a country fair. *"Could you please put my husband Fred in the cheese dome; he has to go in for some tests next week."* Peggy complied. *"I'm so worried about my daughter Nancy, she hasn't phoned home in a month, I hope she's alright."*

Nancy was put in the Cheese Dome. A waitress at a local favorite restaurant handed Peggy her name badge so the Cheese Dome might help her find a new job and she could finally get off her aching feet.

Everyday Peggy passed by her Cheese Dome and watched as it filled with requests for protection and healing. The Cheese Dome took on a life of its own. It became a busy little crystal cathedral sitting on Peggy's kitchen counter watching over all of the people she put in it. And something *was* happening: Frightening growths turned out to be benign cysts, pneumonia was abated, a new job came through and estranged daughters phoned home. Miracles multiplied and news spread. The requests kept coming in as one person told another, and soon Peggy's cheese dome was bursting its bubble top. She thought it might be time to move some of the people out to make room for the new requests. *Not so fast, little lady.*

Peggy quickly learned that people she placed under the dome did not want to be taken out. She would inquire as to how they were doing, hear their positive answers and subsequently ask if she could take them out. "Oh nooooo." Looks of dismay and horror crossed their brows as none wanted to risk being removed from what felt like a miraculous and extremely special place.

They felt so much better about their lives when they were in the protective arms of the healing Cheese Dome, and many of them had experienced affirmative reversals of fortune. No way did they want out of this happening place. Peggy made room for more and the requests poured in. The bits of paper, photographs, badges, buttons, locks of hair and keepsakes were compacted, reorganized and shifted around to make room for the new arrivals. Packed tighter than a starlet's suitcase for a USO tour, the Cheese Dome was filled to the brim. Working around the clock the Cheese Dome pumped out healing after healing and Peggy and her Cheese Dome became quite the celebrities in Vancouver, Washington.

Most all of Peggy's friends and relatives have been in the Cheese Dome at one time or another. The challenges of life, the ups and downs of health, business and romance have landed all of us under there a time or two. In addition to the horrible house story, I can remember a spate of tribulations that would curl the hem of a Cardinal's robe, which landed me in Peggy's Cheese Dome for another extensive, yearlong spell.

Peggy's reassurance that *"this will pass," "things will get better,"* and *"you're going to be all right,"* were comforting in addition to knowing that I was held in the sacrosanct, one of a kind, holy of holies, Cheese Dome. And she was right.

The pains subsided, the divorce was finalized, my heart healed from the betrayal, the overdue bills got paid, the loss of a cherished pet was healed by a new rescue, the house eventually sold, the storms were weathered, and I met the love of my life. I believe it all happened because of the Cheese Dome.

Or maybe that's just how life links up with the passage of time. I'm not sure. I only can attest to the feelings and experience I had while being in Peggy's Cheese Dome. Bottom line is you feel a whole heck of a lot better than you felt before you were put in.

When my Cheese Dome arrived from Peggy, I painstakingly opened the beautifully wrapped gift and saw there, in the middle of layers of tissue, was a most precious and beautiful, sweet little Cheese Dome. (As the tradition went, it was pre-owned and rescued from the shelves of a local thrift store.) I was elated and honored. I felt like I had been passed the Olympic Torch. I had just been voted into the very short list of Cheese Dome members and I embraced it like an Oscar.

As the result of my VIP membership in the club of two, Peggy could now handle the requests from her neck of the woods, and I was appointed to help all of Southern California handle theirs. Peggy did, however, keep my name and my challenges in her Cheese Dome. To this day we keep each other and our respective families in one another's sanctuary. Peggy will always have a special place reserved in my Cheese Dome; and me in hers. It's reciprocal Cheese Doming.

Immediately after receiving my Cheese Dome, I wanted to rush outside and plant a sign out on my front lawn: *Cheese Dome Now Open For Requests*. But I couldn't do it. The neighbors were already leery of my house's new paint job (purple trim), so I dared not do anything else that might upset their apple carts and result in their school marm-like arched eyebrow stares.

Beginning on Christmas Day 1991, I was launched on a journey of Cheese Dome Power that has reached across the globe and back again. The following are true stories of Cheese Dome Power. I hope they will delight, entertain and inspire you.

## Chapter Four: The Inner Workings of the Cheese Dome

In truth, I have no idea how the Cheese Dome really works. But I'm sure the mystery lies somewhere in undiscovered, ancient secrets yet unlocked. The only thing I am sure of is that it *does* work. I've observed the results for nearly two decades now.

Somehow in the action of putting someone and their request under the dome (which is thereby encouraged to  go to work to alter the situation, solve the problem, or improve the condition), magical and unseen powers go to work to affect change. If I knew exactly what it was, I would bottle it, make an infomercial and distribute it to the world. But I don't understand the process thoroughly, I can, however, venture an educated guess.

After many years of using the power of the Cheese Dome to help people, I have arrived at the belief that what you are thinking and what emotion you are feeling when you place names in the dome matters. The love and concern in your heart for the person you are helping, and a sincere belief that the dome is a safe and powerful place, seem to be the initial keys to change. I think that when you write someone's name on a slip of paper, the indiscernible feelings of compassion and care in your heart somehow transfer to the paper.

As you place the paper in the Cheese Dome, the dome contains your genuine empathy and somehow, mysteriously, intensifies it. Under the dome, love and compassion multiply. I like to think of it like the analogy of carbon turning into a diamond; over time, a new reality is created from old stuff. Coal to gemstone; not a bad result for a secondhand Cheese Dome.

There may be, however, some tangible evidence for what occurs in this process. If we consider the slips of paper in the Cheese Dome as a prayer for the person or condition, then we can look to the following research:

*One of the most quoted scientific studies of prayer was done between August of 1982 and May of 1983. 393 patients in the San Francisco General Hospital's Coronary Care Unit, were randomly selected by computer to either receive or not receive intercessory prayer. All participants in the study, including patients, doctors, and the conductor of the study himself remained blind throughout the study.*

*The results of the study are not surprising. The patients who had received prayer as a part of the study were healthier than those who had not. The prayed for group had less need of having CPR (cardiopulmonary resuscitation) performed and less need for the use of mechanical ventilators. They had a diminished necessity for diuretics and antibiotics, less occurrences of pulmonary edema, and fewer deaths. Taking all factors into consideration, these results can only be attributed to the power of prayer.*[3]

---

[3] Williams, Debra, *Scientific Research of Prayer: Can the Power of Prayer Be Proven?*

In response to this study, noted atheist Dan Barker, a spokesperson for the Freedom from Religion Foundation, says the findings of the research are no big surprise. Prayer and religious beliefs can have a placebo effect, just like a sugar pill. Barker, who was once a Christian Fundamentalist preacher before developing serious doubts about his religion, states that one of the strongest factors in recovery from an illness is a sense of connectedness with a community and people who genuinely care about you. Even if we mumble our prayers only when we are ill (or if someone puts them on a piece of paper and slips them under a Cheese Dome), the research indicates that compassionate thoughts, religious or not, could help in healing.

Or maybe it's just magic. At this writing, we simply don't know for sure.
I now believe that Cheese Dome Power is rooted somehow in a mind-body connection and that the thoughts we hold in our mind are transmitted into the dome, magically intensified and sent out to the person in need of healing. How that happens exactly is still a puzzle. But I believe in the power mostly because it continues to work. After all, that's the point.

If something is not effective don't do it; if something is working for you, repeat it. Albert Einstein said, *Insanity is doing the same thing over and over again and expecting different results.* Cheese Dome Power is doing the same thing over and over because you get positive results.

Frankly, I stopped worrying long ago exactly *how* it works and now just concentrate on the fact that it does work for me and for the people I put in it.

Just ask my friend Lisa. She lives in the UK, "over the pond" as we say. One of the most recent emails came in the form of an *urgent* plea to The Cheese Dome Hotline. Here is her story:

*Kac told me about the Cheese Dome quite a while ago, and I was very intrigued by the idea. For some time we've been looking for a new home in the country, so recently my daughter and I created a wish-list describing exactly what we wanted: a little cottage style house (we called it a Hobbit House) on the edge of a small village with good transport links into the city, with a nice garden with a lawn for our dog to play on, and space for us to grow herbs and create a small wildflower meadow, backing onto fields and trees.*

*A few weeks ago, we found the perfect house. It fitted everything on our list, even to small details like an old-fashioned larder in the kitchen. We were thrilled and started making plans to move. Then came a glitch. The people living in the house were unable to leave, due to financial issues. It seemed that we'd have to start looking all over again, and another place as perfect for us, in the area we wanted, was very unlikely to be available. I asked Kac to put us in the Cheese Dome.*

*The following day we were invited to visit the house. We went with heavy hearts, thinking it would just upset us to see it again and not be able to move there. But the Cheese Dome had worked its magic overnight! The current tenants had come up with a solution to their issues, and a date was set for the move in 6 weeks' time.*

*How the Cheese Dome works is a mystery. My feeling is that a lot of love goes in there with the request for help, and the contained energies in the Dome amplify that and create a connection with the tremendous forces of manifestation. Whatever it is that happens within the Cheese Dome, it most certainly works, and I'm hugely grateful to Kac for putting us in there!*

-Lisa Tenzin-Dolma, UK

## Chapter Five: Why A Cheese Dome?

Why a Cheese Dome? Because on several levels, it works. It's hard to lose a Cheese Dome. It's not like a key or a pair of glasses you can easily misplace. It's big, it's attractive and you can't usually miss it. A regular size Cheese Dome can hold a big stack of names and petitions, so it's practical as well as eye catching. Every healer should have one.

"What's that sitting on your counter?" a visitor quizzes after having noticed the domed object on your counter bulging with a collection of paper notes, photos and what not. "Oh that," you reply casually, "it's my Healing Cheese Dome. "Depending on how well the visitor knows you, their facial expressions may vary from "Oh I *seeeee*," to, "What in tarnation are you talking about?" It will be up to you to explain the Cheese Dome, or not, depending on your level of confidence and what kind of mood you're in.

Some pre-rehearsed responses might include:

➢ "Well I'm not really sure how it works. I just know that when I write out a person's name or a troubling issue and put it under the dome, it gets resolved."
➢ "If you had a worry or an illness and you asked me to put your name in my cheese dome, I would, and I know the challenge would pretty much be handled."

> ➤ "I don't worry about things anymore. If something comes up, I put it under the cheese dome and some mysterious forces get together and work it out."
> ➤ "Honey, it beats the heck out of me. I just know the darn thing works."
> ➤ "Would you like to see the one in my car?"

Most of us love to find creative solutions to the challenges of life for ourselves and for our family and closest pals. The desire to help others seems to be innate. "The human heart has a natural desire to help others that comes alive when the need arises."[4] The Cheese Dome then becomes an instrument of our inherent longing to assist one another. It's a tool we can use to express our natural desire to help. "The people who make a difference in your life are not the ones with the most credentials, the most money, or the most awards. They are the ones who care." [5]

Truly then, the compassion that is expressed by finding and using a Cheese Dome creates an opportunity to have a personal miracle maker on your kitchen counter. Momma's little helper. Life presents the challenge that a close friend or loved one is struggling with, we place the person and the problem to be solved inside the Cheese Dome, we walk away, and the healing activity begins.

---

[4] Christian Science Monitor April 2011

[5] Schultze, Charles, www.goodreads.com

As we pass by the Cheese Dome on our daily routine, we are reminded of all the people we care about, the battles they are facing and, with love and compassion for them in our heart, we send out positive thoughts mentally assisting the Cheese Dome in doing its work. Our confidence somehow helps the ju ju congeal and all we have to do is patiently wait for the results and simply trust they *will* occur. At least that's my experience.

It may sound over simplified, but when you think about all of the things, people, newscasts, articles, conversations that can steer you off course - and fill you with negative thoughts of gloom and doom - you'll know that it isn't quite that simple after all. Healing is like having a pet you love. You don't say to your pet one day that you love it and feed it; and then the next day tell it it's not important and withhold its food. No, you know you must remain consistent, even though you may not be entirely thrilled when it chews up your favorite slippers. You still love your pet, even when it leaves a pile of hair behind on your favorite chair. It's the same for the Cheese Dome.

There it sits on your counter reminding you to remain consistent in your belief that it cures, heals, untangles and uplifts whatever you put into it. In spite of what someone else thinks, or tries to make you believe, you remain convinced of what you know to be true.

The Cheese Dome fixes things, people, situations and even, pets. Pets are most welcome in the Cheese Dome. They have their ills, concerns, injuries, frights and their needs, too, can be placed on a slip of paper and slipped under the Cheese Dome to aid them on their journey. I have found that cats have special Cheese Dome radar and they seem to almost smell it in the air when they have Cheese Dome Power behind them.

Back to the Cheese Dome itself. You must not be *married* to the outcome. You can't be. Once you put someone or some situation into the Cheese Dome, you have to let it go and let it adopt a solution and a life of its own. I learned that the hard way.

Once the news of the Healing Cheese Dome got out amongst my friends, I received many requests for the Cheese Dome Solution. Usually the request to be put in the Cheese Dome came with a long story. By the time I listened to the whole story, complete with all the gory details, I had a pretty good sense of how the person felt and what the healing ought to be.

I suppose I wrote down their concerns, problems or issues with a solution in mind: broken heart; mend it fast and find a new love; broken dreams; replace them with a fresh dream and a new passion; broken arm; heal it fast and get the person functioning fully again, a very common and predictable list of hopes for injured friends.

So naturally, when my friend Sandy called and said she had just broken her arm, was in a cast and "would I please put her in the Cheese Dome", I did so immediately; and knew she would heal. Imagine my surprise when a few days later the phone rang and it was Sandy, and she was furious. "You said you were going to put me in your healing Cheese Dome," she yelled. Flustered, I sputtered, "But I did." "Well then, a fine lot of good it did me," she ranted. "I fell and broke my arm in a second place and now I have a cast twice the size." She was sobbing. I was horrified. I glared at the Cheese Dome and said, "What are you *doing*?" The Cheese Dome said nothing. It just sat there. I had a mind to toss it out into the street, but then I remembered all of the good things that had happened for my other friends who'd been placed in it.

So, what was going on? The conundrum raged. For days I walked past the Cheese Dome, snubbed it, blamed it for the new arm break and seriously distrusted the process. I had a giant lapse of faith in the Cheese Dome. Nonetheless, the Cheese Dome Power, as it turned out, was working all along.

When my friend received her second cast she was helped to a waiting car by an accommodating male nurse. He also happened to be on duty when she came back to the hospital to have her cast removed.

In fact, as it turned out, he made sure that he was around for the big event. One smart remark lead to a laugh here and there, which lead to a date, which lead to a romance; and gave us the real reason behind the second break. The Cheese Dome knew what it was doing all along. It was busy healing her entire life by way of her return to the hospital; I was the unbeliever and she was just plain confused. Today we can laugh about it and are grateful for her husband, the nurse.

Since that incident, I have been duly humbled by the perfection in Cheese Dome Power. Far be it for me to second guess the Dome. Nor will I ever again have any attitude against it. The Cheese Dome has its own thing going on. It will embrace whatever or whomever I give it and all will turn out as it should. It doesn't need my (ever so well intentioned) direction. Lesson noted.

Then there was Walli. For many years Walli and I had worked together in the same industry, but never met face to face. She knew my name and I knew hers, but we worked our parallel careers without meeting: until one day. The project I was working on needed a location that Walli's company administrated.

I called her; we had lunch and a fast friendship began. We did business together, shared mutual friends in common and even discovered that we were geographical neighbors - one hill apart- so we socialized on weekends and synchronized our personal and professional lives. Walli recommended me for jobs and I did the same for her.

On a particular day when we met for lunch, Walli was, uncharacteristically, a bit down. The conversation opened up to include her relationship, which I had thought was terrific. Walli revealed that she didn't know what to do because she wanted to get married and her boyfriend hadn't brought up the subject, yet they had been living together for about five years. She questioned whether marriage was even important and wondered if the mere mention of the M word would break them up. She was in a quandary and was second guessing herself. I listened avidly and then suggested we put her and her boyfriend in the Cheese Dome and see what happened.

Walli knew about the Cheese Dome because she had seen it on my kitchen counter many times. Her face brightened at the thought and we both couldn't wait for the outcome. Immediately after returning home I slipped Walli's name under the dome and went on about my day.

About three weeks later Walli called. She was very excited. Hey boyfriend had turned into a fiancé and she couldn't wait to tell me how. I was all ears. Walli was a TV talk show producer and one of the proposed guests was Margaret Kent, author of a book called *How To Marry The Man of Your Choice.*

Walli took the book home on the weekend to read through it before booking the author on the show. As she was out on the patio with a lemonade, her boyfriend joined her and said, "What are you reading?" Walli replied, "We might book this author and I need to know what she has to say." "Oh," he said, and walked away. Thirty minutes later he came back and sat down.

Walli looked up from her book and noticed he clearly had something on his mind. Slowly and deliberately he asked, "Did you want to get married?" She almost fell off her patio chair. Mustering all of the calm she could, while her heart was pounding like a Taiko drum, she replied, "I think that would be nice. How about you?" And he said, "Sure, sounds good."

One of the suggestions in the book, *How To Marry The Man of Your Choice,* suggested that the woman "close the deal" and obtain a commitment for a wedding date as quickly as possible. Walli, with the fresh information in her head, said "How about October?" To which he replied. "Great." Having that out of the way, (a giant sigh was heard around the world) the rest of the steps were easy. A ring was purchased, the banquet room was booked, invitations were ordered, and the wedding was on track. She called to tell me the good news.

We hooted and hollered and shared the joy. Three months later, when all was said and done, I received this postcard from Kauai:

*We're on our honeymoon and with all the planning for the wedding I guess I forgot to say "thank you." I remember the day we had lunch and you so kindly put me in the Cheese Dome. I think about that day as I sit on the beach in Poipu with my husband by my side. I can't believe this has happened. Thank you and thank the Cheese Dome. I never knew I could be this happy. Aloha and Mahalo, Walli.*

# Chapter Six: All Cheese Domes Are Created Equal

You and your Cheese Dome can turn troubles into gifts and situations into solutions. In time, someone may even write a song about the two of you. Allow your relationship to blossom and morph with the times. Remember, "Love is Patient; Love is Kind,"[6] and Love is well expressed in a Cheese Dome.

Cheese Domes work on personal issues, those of friends and family, and even people who come into your circle simply for the purpose of healing. Although you may have made a best friend out of your Cheese Dome, remember that Cheese Dome Power is impersonal. I've learned that it has no favorites and no concern for color, creed or sex and it heals the just and the unjust alike. The real beauty lies in the non-discriminatory nature of its inner workings. It is absolutely bias-free. Cheese Dome Power is the same for all living things, whether in Shanghai or Saskatchewan.

And don't expect to be tuning in next TV season to see the latest hit show, "The Battle of The Cheese Domes," because there is no competition and certainly there are no losers in Cheese Dome land.

---

[6] 1 Corinthians 13:4-7,13

The only question is: if my Cheese Dome is as powerful as King Tut's Cheese Dome, (if he'd had one) because it uses the same invisible energy to accomplish its assignments, then why aren't we all using them? Why aren't we all lining up our Cheese Domes, placing our intentions for healing under the Dome and getting on with the business of creating a better world? Why isn't this a national pastime and why isn't everybody doing it?

Well, they may well do that. This is just the beginning. You are on the cutting edge. We are creating, right here and now as you read this page, a revolution and a culture of Cheese Dome healers that will eventually permeate all walks of life and all facets of society.

I would love to see the day when the President of the United States and various Heads of State around the globe have Cheese Domes sitting on their desks. Each of them will put the problems of the world in the Cheese Dome and allow them to be solved. Taxes? No problem: Cheese Dome. World hunger? No problem: Cheese Dome. Health Care Reform? No problem: Cheese Dome. War? No problem: Cheese Dome. See what I mean?

All in good time. For now, let's just work on our own sphere of influence.

Another thing I've discovered along the Cheese Dome path, is that one Cheese Dome cannot out power another; just as there can be no less power in one Cheese Dome than another. Each holds the same power. What makes the difference in the outcome of Cheese Dome Power lies in the mind of the person placing the message or request under the Cheese Dome. If that person has faith, then the Cheese Dome works on that energy. If, on the other hand, the person placing the request under the Dome has a "show me, chump" attitude, the Cheese Dome will work from that. How do want your Cheese Dome energy to be?

Do you want it working on a positive, supportive, optimistic outcome, or do you want it spending energy overcoming attitude? The choice is in the mind of the placer.

Solving personal issues and challenges is only the first step. When we truly see the effects of the power of the Cheese Dome we can begin to use that power on matters of global concern. I am awed by those possibilities.

As in the case of my friend with the twice broken arm, the Cheese Dome went to work but the outcome was very different than we expected. (You'll remember I was actually mad at the Cheese Dome for a while.) I didn't trust what it was doing; it was only in hindsight that I could see its circuitous path to a solution far better than I, or my friend, could have ever imagined.

In my experience I have learned that the one thing I can rely on is that the Cheese Dome outcome is always good. The Cheese Dome is inherently impersonal, but its natural tendency is to create good for the person or situation placed under its care. We may not appreciate some of the steps in the healing process, as experienced by my friend and the second arm break, but if we trust in the outcome we will find that it is always on the best side of healing.

That healing may come in a different wrapping than we expected, it may look and feel completely unfamiliar, like a set of clothes that are too big or too small for us, but it will come, and it will be exactly what the person or situation needs. A familiar joke can be were written to explain this reaction: "Do you know how to make a Cheese Dome laugh? Tell it *your* plans." Frequently we appreciate the positive results only in hindsight. The Cheese Dome Power does not necessarily always work in our comfort zone; but it always brings healing.

The most powerful manifestation of Cheese Dome healing in my life happened after I learned of my own financial collapse because of the actions of my Financial Advisor. I placed my faith and trust in a high-profile institution and in their agent. After ten years of apparent financial growth, I discovered that the decade was actually filled with lies, fraud, bad investments and an enormous cover up.

The shock of the financial loss was one thing, but the personal betrayal was quite something else. The devastation caused my nervous system to tighten up like the strings on a Rock Star's steel guitar and one day I found myself doubled over in pain at the ER. Diverticulitis was the diagnosis. It was my first physical response to this dark situation. Once I recovered from the internal inflammation I knew I had to figure things out if I was to survive.

I put *the situation* in the Cheese Dome and almost immediately I found a brilliant attorney to handle my case and we got the litigation ball rolling. I had relied on the advice and counsel of my Financial Advisor for so many years, that I had a difficult time believing anyone could be so callous and conniving. I was not alone. As it turned out, there were other victims, too.

After getting through my illness and finding legal representation, I knew I needed a *sit down* with my Cheese Dome. We sat together while I made a list of things that could turn my life around. Ultimately there were six changes, benefits, occurrences and modifications that, if they happened, could mitigate the damage and restore my sanity while I waited for the outcome of my trial. Some items on the list were simple and some were complex. Most of them required a lot of work on my part, but I was willing. I knew that once I committed my list to the Cheese Dome, I had fire behind my plight.

For a solid year I worked on my six changes. I applied for a home modification loan, and it was granted in just six weeks. I reorganized my health insurance plans. I held several garage sales and turned everything I could (that I had been holding onto for too long) into cash. I cracked every piggy bank and looked for hidden treasures in old jewelry cases. I cut back on every expenses (even on heat some chilly days) to save every dime I could.

With my new Financial Adviser, we sold the remaining junk bonds and set on a new course for financial healing. I liquidated, terminated, and revamped everything I owned or held title to and eeeked out enough of a living to get by. I couldn't sell my home and move to a smaller one because the real estate market had dropped so low that I owed more on the property than it was currently worth.

I did everything I could to right the sinking ship and within a year, five of the six things on the list had occurred; making life manageable while the sixth solution percolated. I have no doubt that it will happen. The other five did.

In the extended year of dismal days and sleepless nights, I have to acknowledge the very fact that I entrusted my list of Six Things to the Cheese Dome gave me a sense of strength and hope that I needed to power through the hundreds and hundreds of hours of paperwork and the day after day emotional turmoil or making the five things happen that would improve my life.

I desperately needed both prayer and miracles in my life and the Cheese Dome supplied me with the perfect combination of faith, hope and magic.

## Chapter Seven: Pamela Discovers the Cheese Dome From Oz

My friend Pamela received a midnight call from the hospital near where her parents lived telling her that her mother had died suddenly, from a heart attack.

Pamela had been expecting that her elderly 93-year-old father, who was suffering from heart disease and a lung infection, would be the first one to pass. No one enjoys receiving those kinds of calls, but she was more than shocked to learn that her mother preceded her father and left the planet without warning. Pamela, and her husband Ralph, immediately took off for her parent's home to care for her father and to begin the preparations for her mother's funeral.

The night before the funeral, her father died. After 63 years of marriage he didn't want to be without his beloved bride for another day, so he joined her.

Suddenly orphaned, overnight  Pamela made preparations for the funeral of both her parents.

Dazed by the enormity of the dual loss, Pamela waited a few weeks before attempting the task of sorting through the lifetime of her parents' possessions. Brother Pete joined her, "Going through their belongings with great love and sadness," memories were stirred and moments of raucous laughter were interspersed with immense sorrow and grief.

Among her parents' memorabilia there were pictures of the two of them, the four of them; a lifetime of memories presented in objects and photographs. Her father had been an avid musician and played drums in a band until his 92nd birthday. Her mother was a great organizer. All of the family's memories were right there, filed alphabetically, by date.

As Pamela and Pete were sorting through things the doorbell rang. Pamela went to answer it, but no one was there. Again, the doorbell rang, and Pete went to answer it, and no one was there. This happened repeatedly until Pamela asked Pete if he was doing something weirdly electronic that might be setting off the doorbell. He wasn't. It kept happening until Pete and Pamela could no longer stand it, so Pete "disabled" (which is a nicer way of saying he ripped it off the door) the doorbell and silenced its incessant *ding dongs.* In the back of her mind Pamela wondered if this was some kind of sign.

Shaking off a feeling of "weird," she climbed up on a ladder to reach the uppermost part of the china closet. "My mother was a collector of glassware and commemorative plates," Pamela said, "and what do you suppose I found in her collection? A lovely, bright green, cut-glass cheese dome!" She called me immediately with the news of the discovery and emailed me a picture. We were thrilled. Here her mother had been a closet Cheese Domer for all those years and we didn't know it.

Pamela is now sole heir to the Emerald Cheese Dome from Oz. Well, we figure it must have been from Oz because of the magical way it presented itself to her. Now all I have to do is talk her into some red sequined shoes and get her a dog named Toto, and she'll be all set.

Her journey has begun. Pamela emailed, "OK, maybe it's a covered butter dish but I like the color and the way it catches the light. I think it will be a spectacular addition to the healing network of Cheese Domes, so let me know if you'd like me to put you on a little piece of paper and drop you in."

It just goes to show: You never know when and where a Cheese Dome will find you. Keep your eyes peeled and your heart open.

**Chapter Eight: You and Your New Cheese Dome - the Un-manual**

There is probably a Cheese Dome out there somewhere waiting for you. Maybe it is sitting on the shelf of a local thrift store or it could be on eBay, just waiting for you to spot it or bid on it and bring it home. Wherever it is, if you are meant to have it and be its guardian, believe me, it will find you. The best idea is to find a Cheese Dome that has had an incarnation as an actual cheese keeper. When you rescue it, or adopt it, you give it a second expression of life. The hunt for the perfect candidate is an adventure in itself. So far as I know there isn't a Humane Cheese Dome Society, but we could always start one!

I wouldn't ever presume to tell you what to do with your Cheese Dome once you find it, or when it finds you. For everyone there is a different set of instructions. The only suggestion I can give you is to clean it, decorate it if you choose, and make it uniquely your own. My first Cheese Dome came as a gift, as you know, it wasn't out of the box for more than five minutes when it announced that it wanted its base to be *marbelized*.

How it came to be marbleized is a roundabout story that all began with a dear friend of mine, the actress Shell Kepler from *General Hospital*. Shell possessed an amazing gift for creatively painting the interior of her entire home. Not a square inch escaped her artistic eye and if you stood still long enough around her, you too might find yourself transformed into an art piece.

Her guest bathroom was a masterwork. One entered it under a blossoming bough of wisteria tumbling across the top of the entrance arch reaching well into the inner sanctum of the powder room. Additional extensions of cascading flowers summoned you further into a three-dimensional sumptuous carnival of flora. One definitely had the feeling that you had been instantly teleported to an Italian country villa in springtime.

Her dining room escorted you into a mystical Arabian Sunset with splashes of color stolen from desert sands. Framed by hand dyed pastel gauze curtains, the room was alive with the enticing mysteries of the Far East.

No white wall was safe from Shell's imagination. In fact, she saw each one as a personally engraved invitation to her symphonic palette of paints. I caught the bug from her. I was bitten by the deep desire to make every room in my house outstanding and unique.

Decades prior, I had taken an art class in college and vaguely remembered how to layer paint one color over another, using sponges. As my class project I had successfully painted a footstool that resembled malachite when I was finished. Falling back into a familiar comfort zone, my first foray into palatial wall painting began with a sea sponge and four colors of glaze. Buoyed by Shell's infectious élan, I launched into my first wallscape.

I wanted to make my dining room look like it was in a Tuscan estate. After the first hour, I had accomplished only 2 square feet of faux Tuscan texture. The room had well over 1,000 square feet of wall space, so my progress was deeply disappointing and by my calculations, I would be finished with the room sometime after Christmas. This was July. I was discouraged, so I made a call.

Shell came to my rescue. Always gracious, she did not burst out laughing when she eyed the paltry progress. Instead, she suggested we immediately paint over the spot I had worked so industriously on, which took a total of 10 minutes (including opening and stirring the old wall paint,) and begin anew.

With Shell at the helm, we rolled on a base coat a little this way, some more that way and ever more hither and yon. Before the paint had time to dry, we tossed wet rags up and slid them down the walls on sticks.

Then, with spray bottles in hand we created "weathering" using strategically placed mists of water and, while still soaking wet, we coated with walls with another paint roller textured with plastic bags tied around the core and applied to the walls haphazardly (or perhaps I should use the word "randomly"?).

We enjoyed a glass of champagne while the walls dried a tad and applied yet one more coat of a darker color using a combination of oven mitts, a floor mop and a moth-eaten shammy.

We accomplished the re-facing of the entire room in less than four hours, including our champagne break. We still had time left over to cook and our husbands joined us for dinner in our freshly painted Tuscan dining room. *Viva Italia!* My artistic side was stoked.

When the Cheese Dome arrived that Christmas, the plain wooden base would not be silenced. The Cheese Dome "spoke" to me as only a Cheese Dome can and convinced me it needed to have a marble-looking base, a *purple*, marbleized base no less. I acquiesced. I procured my sponges from the basement along with a selection of purple and lavender paints and began with a layer at a time.

To my surprise and delight it actually looked like purple marble. I finished it off with a topcoat of clear gloss. The Cheese Dome instantly became a personalized masterpiece, and all dolled up, it was ready to be engaged.

At least once a week the phone rang with someone requesting Cheese Dome support. Since the day it was called into action, the Cheese Dome has never been idle.

When you find your Cheese Dome, I strongly suggest that you initiate a conversation with it and be open to hearing what it has to say.

I don't know about you, but I talk to things all the time. It started by talking to plants, "grow" I would say, and they did. Of course, I talk to my pets, the squirrels and the birds outside and I've been known to hold a conversation or two with glassware, especially when one of them jumps out of the cupboard and crashes onto the floor.

I'll even admit to talking to a clothes dryer (which is usually a plea not to shrink something I entrust to it). So far I haven't been locked up for having chats with inanimate objects. If you don't think you have the same type of conversations - just pay attention to the next time you stub your toe, or an appliance works too slowly.

Your new Cheese Dome may speak to you, as mine did, about appearance, or it may desire a specific location. It knows what its job is, so the best thing you can do is to let it have its say. If I thought of it as a child of mine, I would be inclined to tell it what to do. But, if I considered it more like a niece, a nephew, or a Godchild I would tend to be more flexible, and probably spoil it a bit. Once you and your Cheese Dome have gotten to know each other, you'll know instinctively the exact moment to begin giving it assignments.

As a first step you might consider putting the first piece of paper in it with something you want to heal or change in your life. Write it out, place it in the Dome and release it. Go on with your life but observe when the changes begin to emerge.

Write your request in a positive sentence
as if it was already true.

**The Ten Things You Absolutely Want To Do With Your Cheese Dome:**

- ➢ Personalize it through your artistic expression and talents. (This may involve, glue, rhinestones, paint, feathers, puffy paint or whatever your wild imagination can conjure up and your art supply store carries.)The sky is the limit when it comes to creativity.
- ➢ Allow it to tell you where *it* wants to call *home*. Here's where that conversation between you and the Cheese Dome comes in handy. You will know for sure after you try a few locations around your home as the Cheese Dome will pick the most favorable one and let you know.
- ➢ Spend a few moments with it every day. Cheese Domes get lonely, too. Don't ignore it.
- ➢ Praise it and encourage it. A kind word and appreciation go a long way with a Cheese Dome. Every Cheese Dome loves flattery and attention. Be generous with your compliments and conversation.
- ➢ Greet it with a smile. Remember that it's always hard at work; a smile helps (and it won't hurt you either).
- ➢ Keep it clean and sparkling. Like fine jewelry, it is more dazzling when kept free of dust and kitchen grease.
- ➢ Add new items to it as often as you want. In the Cheese Dome, the more the merrier. It can never be too full or have too many requests. It thrives on volume.

➢ Talk freely about it and allow people to ask questions. Remember that the Cheese Dome helps people heal and situations work out for the best, always. It accomplishes what you ask. Trust in the outcome.
➢ Love it. Treat it like the dear friend and helper it is. It only wants the best for you and your highest good.

## The Ten Things You Never Want To Do With Your Cheese Dome:

➢ Don't rush the process. (You wouldn't rush out into the garden and pull on the shoots to make the plant grow faster, would you? Same with the Cheese Dome; it has its own process and takes the time it needs to solve the problems it's been given. Be a good boss and allow it time to complete its assignment.)
➢ Don't allow it to be used as a toy. (Healing is serious business.)
➢ Don't criticize it. (Awwwww...you'd never do that, would you?)
➢ Don't challenge it. (Pick on someone your own size.)
➢ Don't threaten it. (see above)
➢ Don't doubt it. (Always keep the faith; the Cheese Dome will prevail.)
➢ Don't negate it. (Don't be a nag. Follow that" flies to honey" adage.)
➢ Don't give up on it. (Cultivate patience and trust in the process)

> Don't punish it. (Never call it *naughty*, spank it or give it a *time out*.)
> Don't hurt its feelings. (Cheese domes have feelings too!)
> Don't hide it. (There is no shame in having, or being, a Cheese Dome. Display it proudly.)

The Cheese Dome will become a part of your life; it has joined your family for a reason. It has sought you out to create a beautiful partnership. Your part is to attract the people and situations that need help from the Healing Cheese Dome. When you write down the name or the situation and place it in the Cheese Dome sincerely believing that it will be healed, the Cheese Dome will go to work. Your job is to introduce the Cheese Dome to the challenge and the Cheese Dome's job is to take it from there to the highest good. Together you can change the world one person and one challenge at a time.

## Chapter Nine: Putting the Cheese Dome to Work

The helping, healing Cheese Dome is an all-purpose solution to life's challenges and speed bumps. If you're wondering how to put it to the best use just consider these questions:

> - What is the biggest problem facing you today?
> - What may have created the problem?
> - What thinking may have created or contributed to the problem?
> - What needs to change for there to be a solution?
> - Are you open to the idea that there may be a solution that you haven't thought of?
> - Are you willing to let the Cheese Dome handle it?

> Now you're ready to write out the situation and, trusting that only the greatest good will come about, slip it under the Cheese Dome for fulfillment. Cheese Dome Power for all!

This is just the beginning! You have a new life ahead.

**More Books From
Dr. kac young**

**Discover Your Spiritual Genius**
A compendium of helpful shortcuts for your spiritual development. This is the beginner's guide to knowing it all. You need this book if you're feeling down in the dumps or if your life isn't working the way you want it to. If you read and follow this advice life will take on a new meaning, you will be on top of your game, in charge of your life, happier, and more fulfilled.

**Feng Shui, the Easy Way**
The ancient art from China that can change your life overnight. This is a shortcut to proven Feng Shui principles and practices which can create immediate results in your life. Harmonize your life by balancing the "stuff" in it. It's easier than you think. The results are life-altering for the good.

**Dancing With the Moon**
Learn how to use the natural energies of the lunar forces to orchestrate your life, your emotions and to create a deeper experience of living life at its fullest measure. Dancing With the Moon is easy to learn and simple to use. You will be enriched daily with this process. There is nothing more healing than living in rhythm with the lunar phases.

**Chart Your Course**  - online only
http://chartyourcourse12.com/

Create the year you want and fulfill your dreams by working with the energies of the stars and the planets. You can create the life you have always wanted by following these 12 simple steps to harness the cosmic energies that are just out there waiting for you. It's a process that will change your inner life and manifest what you truly want to have in your outer life.

**The Healing Art of Essential Oils**
A wonderful introduction to the art of using essential oils with lots of recipes and profiles for 50 oils. Brilliant book for the beginner or advanced user. Highly recommended by experts.

**The Art of Healing with Crystals**, a wonderful book that explains all about crystal energies and how you can use them to help yourself emotionally, physically and spiritually.

**The One Minute Cat Manager, Sixty Seconds to Shangri-La**. This book is a wonderful romp through cat companionship and shows you how you can manage a cat no matter how busy you are with these 60 second ideas. Delightful stories and entertaining drawings make this book a must-have. Bedtime stories for cats will delight you and kitty. Practical information will help you understand your cat and deepen your bond.

**Natural Healing for Cats Combining Bach Flower Remedies and Behavioral Therapy,** The gentle way to help your feline friends. This book outlines which Bach Flower Remedy is appropriate for what feline condition. It's a force-free way to assist cats and change unwanted behaviors. Use this gentle way to help your cats heal, cope and adjust to life with humans.

**Gold Mind** is a book about managing your finances, learning about money management and creating your personal wealth one paycheck at a time. This book will change your thinking about money and help you increase your prosperity. Highly recommended by financial experts.

**Supreme Healing** is a Master guideline to healing. No matter what you want to heal in body, mind or spirit, you can use this book as your ladder to success. It contains all the thinking and processes you'll ever need to heal yourself.

**The Ultimate Guide to Crystals for Healing and Beyond.** This is the intermediate book on crystal healing, techniques and combinations with essential oils, crystals, chakras, astrology, archetypes and the 12 Laws of Karma for deep and effective healing. If you want to heal yourself or are a healer, this book is a must-have for your practice and library.

**The Quick Guide to Bach Flower Remedies**. If you've ever wondered how Bach Flowers work, you need this book. It is designed to give you a quick, thorough and easy reference for the use and effectiveness of Bach Flowers. You can heal by just looking at the paintings of each flower. It is exquisite and full of vibrational healing ideas and techniques. Purchase at: https://www.kacyoung.com/product/bach-flower-remedies/ The book is NOT available on Amazon

VISIT www.kacyoung.com for more information on each book.

www.ingramcontent.com/pod-product-compliance
Lightning Source LLC
Chambersburg PA
CBHW071019040426

42443CB00007B/856